THE ANGELIC HOST BRING THEIR INDIVIDUAL SERVICES FOR HUMANITY'S BLESSING

Stevie Lee Honaker, Ph.D.

BALBOA.
PRESS
A DIVISION OF HAY HOUSE

Balboa Press books may be ordered through booksellers or by contacting:

Balboa Press
A Division of Hay House
1663 Liberty Drive
Bloomington, IN 47403
www.balboapress.com
1 (877) 407-4847

Because of the dynamic nature of the Internet, any web addresses or links contained in this book may have changed since publication and may no longer be valid. The views expressed in this work are solely those of the author and do not necessarily reflect the views of the publisher, and the publisher hereby disclaims any responsibility for them.

The author of this book does not dispense medical advice or prescribe the use of any technique as a form of treatment for physical, emotional, or medical problems without the advice of a physician, either directly or indirectly. The intent of the author is only to offer information of a general nature to help you in your quest for emotional and spiritual well-being. In the event you use any of the information in this book for yourself, which is your constitutional right, the author and the publisher assume no responsibility for your actions.

Any people depicted in stock imagery provided by Thinkstock are models, and such images are being used for illustrative purposes only. Certain stock imagery © Thinkstock.

Printed in the United States of America.

ISBN: 978-1-4525-1993-7 (sc)
ISBN: 978-1-4525-1992-0 (e)

Library of Congress Control Number: 2014914066

Balboa Press rev. date: 11/05/2014

Contents

Beloved ones, I am Ascended Master Lord Lanto, Chohan of the Second Ray of God's Light, the golden Ray of Wisdom. I have come to bless this work for humanity. Many of mankind is in great need of the words of the Angels; their love and assistance and a defined way to call them.

I also bless mankind with the assurance the words of God through the Angels will bring the truth of life to everyone. This work has been developed by God through His Angelic Host to bring His love, His wisdom and His will for mankind to read and to learn how to call the Angelic Host and request their loving services for every individual who chooses to call their presence closer to them.

It is God's desire mankind call the Angels. The one who chooses to call is invited to see what the Angels will do for them, if they will just acknowledge each Angel by its name and request their assistance in using the words given at the end of each Angel's writing. Every individual is free to ask as many Angels as they care to for their assistance. There is no limit to the number of Angels you can call, if you will acknowledge them by name with a sincere heart and a willingness to open your mind to unlimited possibilities.

It is my sincere hope every soul will avail themselves to test the validity of this Book and the Angelic Host with their heartfelt requests to the Angels who are waiting for their calls. My love and singular gratitude to God, the One of All for allowing the Angelic Host to manifest this loving work for all mankind.

I am Lord Lanto, Chohan of the Second Ray, the Wisdom of God

Dear one, I am Ascended Master Lady Leto. My Light is white with God's inspiration to live a life full of service. My purpose, directed to me by God, the Supreme Being of All Life is to bless mankind with the higher calling of service to others. I am His continuous and constant servant to the Light given by God to the world of mankind.

It is God's intention we serve in a way that blesses others and their lives, rather than merely living only choosing to serve the self and its lower desires of the five physical senses. Most choose the later and in doing so spend countless lives gaining little spiritual growth. Progress requires lives of dedicated service for the betterment of mankind in some altruistic activity over one's life. In service to others, one actually betters oneself more than the assistance they gave to others. That is God's Law of Reciprocation and it is full of blessings to the one wise enough to engage it in their lives.

If you are seeking to free yourself from only satiating your physical senses and want to permanently be released from the wheel of life, I can assist you. I request Ascended Master Lady Leto to assist and release the physical body's hold on my lifestream until I am completely free in God's magnificent Light and love eternal. I ask to be enfolded with the white Light of God which will inspire me to help others and bless my life expediently and greatly beyond my former expectations for my life.

At your call and spoken request, I will come instantly to bless you with God's inspirational white Light. Call on me as often as you like. I will surround your being with the inspiration of God with my all encompassing love for you. As God's perfect creation, you are eternally held in the highest esteem by all who have contributed to this gift from God. May you use it wisely to the betterment of your life by serving others well.

Beloved, I am Archangel Gabriel. My Light orb is violet with pink at the outer edges. I am directed by God to bring messages to those that wait upon the Lord. I am here to tell you of Great Happenings. The world is waiting for God's Angels to show them the way home. We, the Angels of God are speaking to them through our words written in this Book for you to read and call; to ask and receive our loving assistance for every request.

It is our great joy to share our names, the color of our Light in service to humanity, as well as our particular areas of service and problems we can solve with the reader's sincere acknowledgment and gratitude. We have presented many Angels. Every Angel has varying colors of God's Light, differing services and their own area of healing. In order to better acquaint mankind with who we are, specifically what we can do and how every one can avail themselves of our immediate and loving assistance, we have written for your daily use to allow us into your hearts and minds to love you as you truly are: God's perfect creation.

Now, we call upon you to set aside a brief time every day to open these writings created for you by God's loving direction to the Angels to reach closer than ever before to assist every one of humanity. We hope you will call upon us; the Angels of God created just for humanity's wellbeing, so we may be allowed to come into your life with God's healing love. We can be present with you the moment you speak our name. We will stay with you until your request is fulfilled, as long as you continue to have faith in God, faith in our assistance and our ever present love continuously with you.

I am Archangel Gabriel

Dearest one, I am Archangel Gissel. My Light is white. My purpose is to enfold mankind with the Light of God to assist all in humanity who are trusting God completely in their lives. When one reaches a point in their spiritual life where they truly realize God is omnipotent, they begin to reach out to God in a deeper trust.

Once these calls to God begin, which demand the power of God to come into the physical octave to overcome all matter of strife in human creation, I am directed to enfold and to surround the caller with God's all powerful love and protection for them and their immediate surroundings. When there is a spark of increased Light within the physical realm, the Light of God instantly flashes there continuously to protect and expand this Light. With every call or prayer given, the Light increases within the individual and also goes instantly to where it is called or does as it is directed, as long as the call is constructive and within the will of God for all life.

If you have decided to give daily calls, in order to open the doors of heaven so more of God's Light is able to continuously stream into the physical with permission of your free will, begin with calling Me, Archangel Gissel. Ask for My white Light of God's love, which is the greatest power in all of creation to come in and around you continuously as you speak your calls or give your prayers. I will instantly flash God's protecting love to enfold you and your immediate surroundings. Please call Me and I will joyously be with you in any circumstance to assist you with God's all powerful love.

I am Archangel Gissel

Greetings! I am Thor, an Archangel among the seraphim of God, the Highest come to introduce the Angels of the seraphim for the glory to God. We wish to introduce each of Us as individual spheres of Light and the love of God for His creation. We come in loving service, reaching every one with joy and a willingness to answer every call. Let us begin in the protection of God's encircling Light and love for all.

As Archangel Thor, I express My individuation of God's Life as an orb of crystal blue, as in the color of a clear blue sky. My energy consists of the will of God. With this energetic imprint, My purpose is to assist each one seeking to determine God's will for them in all subjects relating to their daily life, as well as direction for their spiritual life. In their every situation, problem or condition, I assist the one who asks, what is the will of God for me? The will of God always begins with love and I point to the ways His love can be brought into all their concerns.

With the thought of Archangel Thor and My blue Light, I am instantly present and ready to bless every one. The requests for God's love, wisdom and power are a choice for His will and love to express in each concern they give to Me.

God's loving will to all, Archangel Thor

Salutation to all, I am Alohim, Archangel of the seraphim come to bless all with My orb of Light, shimmering in golden hues from God. I wish to serve God by helping humanity asking for Angels to come close to their little ones: the children. My purpose is to protect all new life, especially newborns and toddlers, as you call them.

My golden Light from God is centered within their hearts at conception, so the child constantly feels the immense love of God during this time. After their birth, I surround their bodies with love and protection, as I constantly tell them, "You are God's love." I am with them until they take their first step. Other Angels have been with them assisting and protecting every precious life as it begins it short stay on earth. We serve together in harmony for the good of each child.

Calling for Me often, even before the child is born, brings My presence and golden Light closer with your acknowledgement of My love and care. Think of the glorious golden Light cast with the first rays of sunrise to capture My Light in your mind. Feel this loving Light surrounding your being and babe with all the love of God. We of the Angelic Host know only God's perfect love and serve joyously to all who call on Us.

Placing God's golden Light around all, I am Archangel Alohim

Dear one, I am of the seraphim known as Archangel Shanuel. My orb of Light is colored with the tint of blue, as in the robin's egg. My purpose is to serve mankind at the time of passing from the human form to the Light of their eternal being, once other Angels have helped the light body to be free from the physical form. They carry and direct each Soul to join with the seraphim to once again hear the music of the spheres. The godly melodious sound of love is all healing as it lifts their energy further from the density of the physical cloak.

Thinking of or calling the seraphim, at your request to come closer or assist is always honored. For whatever you need that is constructive, We will answer and if you are troubled, We hold the love you asked for until you are peaceful and can receive all the blessings held in your request.

Please be assured what humans call death is temporary and but a gentle passing of the Soul in its journey of ascension to live and move within the infinite love of the one supreme eternal life. Many Angels are present with you now as you read, gently surrounding you in God's love, singing or whispering with joy, "You are God's perfection."

Dearest one, know and let yourself feel in your heart that all are cared for every moment with infinite love and as many Angels as you call to be present with you and those you love.

Archangel Shanuel

Dearest one, I am Archangel Angela. My orb is sparkling white with violet at the outer edge. My purpose is to bring the presence of God to all who seek Him. You can feel My presence by your side when you call.

My service to all humanity is to gently wrap them in the loving white Light of God whenever they call for Light. Light gives life to all and God's Light enfolded around you blesses everyone with feelings of peace or in other words, all in my world is okay, safe and sound; held so by God's Light and love.

Visualize white lilies and think of their golden center parts as the golden sun of God within you. White lilies are used at Easter in mankind's world. For the realm of the Angels, the white lily symbolizes the arisen Christ at His ascension within all His Light and glory. The next time you see a lily notice how their shape lifts up from the stem and opens wide to reveal their golden stamens and pistol reaching to the sky. The color of the Christ Light is dazzling golden Light.

When you want to feel the presence of God, remember the white lily in all its glory and ask the seraphim Angels to bless you and your loved ones with the gentle, all loving Light of God. We come instantly at your call with love in Our hearts to serve all humanity with His glorious presence.

I am Archangel Angela

I am Archangel Silvanel. My Light orb is white with silver glistening throughout. My purpose is to assist all who ask for purification of their bodies. When given a request from humanity, I am there with them in an instant to assist with their needs for themselves or others.

My service to God, the Supreme Perfect One is to lift the density of human energy, when requested and given permission, out of the human body. After a difficult event, humans create a tremendous, thick energy in and around the body which continues to hold there in a smoky cloud or fog, as it appears from Our perspective. My purpose is to purify this dense energy, so that the body's natural aura can return to it natural state.

After calling for My presence with you, think of yourself sitting among white clouds. As you rest there, feel a soft mist falling gently around you. Feel the effervescent energy of pure Light enfold you in its sparkling essence of God's life. I am happy to be with you and the loved ones that come into your mind. See them also, enfolded in the silvery, glistening mist of My purification until all is Light around them. Thank you for allowing Me to bring the perfection of God into your physical world this day.

I am with you in God's perfect love, Archangel Silvanel

Dearest one, I am Archangel Celia. My Light is white. My purpose is to bring illumination to the hearts and minds of those seeking God with the Light of God's Illumination. When each person begins to seek the creator within, I am there to assist the process of discovery.

Seeking your Creator for His illumination will bless your life exceedingly more than you can imagine. This process is worth your effort and thought to consider every truth presented.

To illuminate the mind entails clearing the collection of unnecessary thoughts, ideas and concepts which no longer serve them. In doing so, the way is opened for new, higher ways of thinking to emerge. The way is cleared for more of God's Light to enter and remain.

The effect of this clearing out the old and bringing in God's Light is enormous. The Light affects every area. Not only is the mental level cleared, Light's effect reaches through the body and the entire energetic body for the clearing and uplifting of all. This means every cell in the physical body receives the tremendous effect from the Light's presence.

Call on Me when you seek illumination. My service for you will bring new energy, perspective and inspiration to your quest. Think of the soft glow of candlelight as My color, as you call for My presence to be with you. Feel a gentle, warm peace surrounding your mind. I come instantly to alleviate your concerns. My presence with you will bring peace and a new confidence to find that which you most seek.

I am Archangel Celia, joyful to be of service in your most important quest to know your God within

Dearest one, I am Archangel Sila. My orb of God's Light is pink. My purpose is to instill the love of God into the hearts of those who wish to be compassionate and merciful to those around them. When asked, I surround their hearts with the love of God and hold the peace of acceptance from His wonderful Light and love in the hearts of others. Blessing others in this holy way allows blessings to come your way. Judging and criticizing others delays the blessings coming to you.

Each moment God sends more blessings to all of His creation. If your heart is right with God, you are able to receive these blessings. Enfolding others with your love will open the door of their hearts to receive God's continuous blessings. With this act of love, you will have changed their life forever. No matter how their outer life appears, their inner life with God has changed for the better. Love is faithful to this truth of life.

I am with you when you call Me by My name, Archangel Sila. Then, request My assistance by bringing My Light to surround you completely. Feel My pink Light glow in your heart. See it glowing in the hearts of others you love or encounter. Hold the peace of God in your heart that all is well. Ask for My presence to be with you anytime, dear one. I am there at your call to enfold you and all you include within the love of God which blesses all every moment.

I am Archangel Sila

Greetings, I am of the seraphim of the Angelic Host. You may call Me Archangel Sophia. My Light orb is green. My purpose is to heal the hearts of mankind. Human life places great strain upon the heart with fears, worries and the stresses of the present. I come when called to surround the heart with Archangel Raphael's powerful green healing Light from God. When acknowledged and requested this Light envelopes and flows through the physical heart and heart center to release all discordant creation held there and allows the heart area to clear and return to its natural state.

For ones who have had heart surgery, calling in My Light will allow the heart and body to heal. Others may call for My healing Light for those you know or love that are experiencing difficulties in their heart area. Although there are unlimited numbers of Healing Angels within the Angelic Host which serve to heal all bodily difficulties, I am consecrated to focus God's love into the physical heart area only. We are closer to God's love expanding for all. I will serve humanity by directing God's love to the heart center of all mankind, if requested to do so.

Think of the fresh, new leaves of Spring to envision My orb of Light, as you call Me closer to heal those you love, know or yourself. I am always here waiting for your permission to surround the hearts of mankind with God's perfect healing Light and love. We with God's love will come instantly bringing blessings and healing to all who call to expand God's healing to all of humanity.

I am Archangel Sophia.

Dear one, I am Archangel Emanuel. My orb of Light is violet. My service is to raise the vibration of the causal level around the human body. I do this by sending the Light to envelope the entire energetic field. As the Light instantly moves throughout the aura and physical body, all discordant energy created by the individual will be transmuted into God's perfect, living life essence.

Humans create with their feelings and thoughts an imprint of discord upon life which qualifies the perfect substance with the imperfect creation of their emotions and thinking. Without intentions continuously centered on God first, humanity mistakenly creates continuous discordant energy around them. As a result this discord also creates in their outer experiences problems, challenges and ill health which God's perfect love will not allow.

Only through acknowledgement and calling to the violet Angels of consuming love, can the discordant energy be removed and reconstituted into the purified, perfect living life essence. We, the violet Angels, wait and patiently long for humanity's call to free them from the mass of discordant energy that surrounds them. When requested, God's love blasts the mistaken energy into instant perfection. You should request daily this purification, in order to maintain your godly connection to Light. Feel free to ask more than once a day for purification, as We love to serve God's Light and humanity in this way.

Envision a violet Light enveloping your feet and gently rising up around your body and over your head. You will feel warmth as love enfolds your being in the Light. We invite you to ask for Our presence to be with you often!

I am violet Archangel Emanuel

Dearest one, I am Nathan. My Light is iridescent white. My purpose is to come to mankind, when called, to lift the veil of all deceit and error from their minds and bodies. My white Light instantly eradicates the confusion and chaos left in their system by the use of drugs. I have assisted mankind with this problem for eons in other civilizations known and unknown to man. The small world of the five senses misuses the chemicals of the elements to falsely enlarge their world and experience. By doing so, they create a horrible imbalance in the mind and body, also creating horrendous thought forms and giving their energy to the psychic.

My Light absorbs and annihilates all that is not of the Light. In one flash of My Light, years of drug use creations are swept away, so Healing Angels may come. Then, the true recovery may begin. We are always available to help the individual, when called, to stay in recovery. A long period is required for humans to return to health. We assist every step of the way continuing to clear their minds, bodies and energetic aura of every creation that is not of the Light.

As you can see, there is an Angel for every problem mankind can create. Know We only love the individual and see them always as God created them: perfect.

See My white Light surrounding anyone you know with this problem and I will instantly clear, illuminate their mind, heal their body of cravings and fill their being with Light. God is always with them.

I am Archangel Nathan

Greetings, I am Angel Terrafenel of the seraphim. My orb of Light is green. My purpose is to assist those who want to help heal planet earth. In this time of her great distress, all of those in body who are also concerned about her condition and are helping in many different ways to heal her are the recipients of My Light.

When mankind calls My Light closer to them, I assist the action of everyone on behalf of earth's health and ascension. With so much population and injury to the planet, it is difficult for earth to maintain its balance, in order to support all life.

Call on Me when you are beginning your work whatever that may be and I will increase your energy and make things go smoothly, so much more may be accomplished. Even the smallest of acts, such as recycling, composting and walking more instead of driving your car will make a large difference.

If you choose, I will inspire you with more ideas of how to help earth heal. You can ask Me anytime, by just thinking of Me and My green Light. Then, I am able to surround, inspire and help you to do even more and better things that will heal the earth even faster.

I am Angel Terrafenel

Dearest, I am Angel Danuel. My orb of Light is white. My Light is dedicated to expanding the love of God wherever I find its Light in the hearts of humanity. Whenever a human is expressing the feelings of love, in the form of care or concern for another, I can be called there to expand the loving energy.

In expanding the love expressed, the people involved receive the full effect of it without energetic interference from any negativity around them or in the atmosphere around them. I make sure they receive the love intended for them.

The love expressed by humans coming from the heart for their families and friends is very important for each to receive. This love, amplified by God's love is a true blessing that must reach the heart of the receiver. That is what I do. I make sure all the feelings of love safely reach the heart, as intended.

Once the love sent has completely reached the heart, this loving energy is transferred to the blood as it moves through the heart spreading this love throughout the body. The expanding love has a calming and healing effect as it circulates through the entire system.

The next time you feel love for another or want to send love to distant family or friends, please remember to call on Me to expand your love and see that it completely reaches the hearts of those you love.

I am Angel Danuel

Dear one, I am Angel Gabel. My orb of Light is white. My purpose is to bless humanity with God's white Light when humanity is suffering from fear. I see the growth of fear around an individual or group of people. I come in an instant when an Angel is thought of by anyone anytime when they are feeling fear.

My Light absorbs the fear and releases humanity from all fear. Fear tries to keep mankind in prison, so humanity cannot live the life God intended for them to have. Fear is a part of the sinister force battling with the Souls of mankind in the balance; however, only God's love and Light can and will defeat the temporary force of evil. I am One of the trillions and trillions of the Angelic Host unlimited in number which have been created by God to love and protect humanity from all harm. It is Our greatest joy to be called into the physical octave by any person needing Our help. We flash the power of God's Light whenever acknowledged and asked to extinguish fear and all of its effects on humanity.

You can think of My white Light and that is all that is needed to call Me close to your side and your loved ones. To instantly dispel all fear you can send My white Light to anyone filled with fear in the world. Places you see or hear about where destruction is causing fear, please call for the white Light of God to annihilate all fear, so the Angels of white Light have the free will permission from you to instantly flash God's all powerful Light into the darkness. This is the only way mankind can be freed from all wars, destruction and chaos on the earth.

I am Angel Gabel

Dear ones, I am Shamuelioné. My Light is pink. My purpose is to unite children that have been separated at birth by the mistakes made from others around them. Through events, accidents, crime, disasters and wars so many people, especially children are affected by the human creation of discord which can cause mistakes to be made in hospitals.

It is My joy to find them in the chaos and seek the fastest way to bring each to safety and reunited with family or others who will care properly for them. Often, it is only a matter of prayer from someone to engage My service in the Light that the missing person will be found or returned. Other complications may arise that prevent their return until many years later. However, once I am called to assist, the Light of God is ever constant to restore the balance of life.

Call on Me when you see or hear of a report of a missing child or person, so My Light can instantly surround them. I hold them in the Light keeping them calm and seek ways to help them return, if it is allowed in their soul contract. If they have deemed, while in Spirit, that another outcome takes their Soul closer to God, I obey their wishes of free will. It is difficult for those left behind to understand all that is involved. There are Angels to comfort those left on earth and give them peace which are the Angel of Peace who come instantly when called.

Call on Me when you need My special help for you, someone you know or some situation you come to know about. I will instantly wrap them in God's Light and hold them through to their highest good in God's wisdom.

I am Angel Shamuelioné

Dear one, I am Angel Faruel. My orb of Light from God is shimmering white with violet around the outside of My orb. My purpose is to assist individuals with the opening of their inner eye, so they can see the Angels and Cosmic Beings inside their mind's eye.

When My Light is acknowledged and called to come close, I am instantly there with them to answer their call for My assistance. I help align the inner sight organs in the brain, so God's Light travels through them. In doing so, the inner sight is attuned to the Light of God.

It is important to dedicate one's inner sight to the service of God's Light as its only use. One must use the inner sight for constructive purpose and for your closer contact with God. Any other use will create untold atonement and discord upon one's life for many embodiments to come, in order to atone for your mistakes and any harm done to others.

You may call on Me by thinking of My orb of white and violet Light coming into your forehead and resting there as you meditate on the Light and love of God in your mind, throat and heart chakras. I will come to heal and hold God's Light as you request for the opening of your inner sight.

In God's service, I am Angel Faruel of the Angelic Host always serving the Light of God's inner sight for mankind's ascension in the Light

Greetings, I am Archangel Teapolius. My orb of Light is sparkling crimson. My purpose is to assist those in need of help with their supply and their survival on earth. My service in the Light of God is to open new avenues of resources to come to them more easily. Survival is not an issue of the fittest. It is a matter of allowing God's abundance to flow into your life by loving Him and choosing to serve God always with the highest and best action you know in your heart to do. If one will get their heart right with God, all His love provides will care for all the earthly needs required to live.

My purpose then is to assist each individual to seek God in their hearts. When they do this, I will open every blessing from God for them that has been held in keeping by the Angels. I make sure they receive God's love in abundance, as long as they keep their hearts attuned to Him. This is Gods divine plan for each in His creation to live a happy and fulfilled life. It is mankind's choice to turn away from God's love and blessings. God does not punish or ever withhold His opulent love for His children.

If you are in need, if your loved ones are in need or you know of others anywhere in the world suffering from lack and struggling to survive, call on Me to assist. Think of My crimson Light surrounding those in need, illumining their minds to be receptive to God in their hearts. Instantly, I am at their side placing hope in their minds and God's love in their hearts to encourage, strengthen them and open God's sources to flow in them and to them from above. If they will keep God in their hearts with gratitude for all of His love for them, even more blessings will continue to flow to them for their constructive use. That is the law of God's love for all of His creation.

I am Archangel Teapolius

Dearest one, I am Archangel Sarah of the seraphim. My Light orb is a pearlescent white with soft blue on the outside edge of My Light. My purpose is to help those in need of additional love in the area of planning their life's work and career. My love from God is sent to them to encourage and strengthen their search for what to do to earn their living. I inspire and give them the courage to try out new interests and explore the possibilities open to them. My Light increases their desire to change, a sometimes difficult action for humans to take.

In doing so many doors of opportunity open for them to search, in order to find activities they like to do. This is a process that takes time and patience with oneself. It is important to consider your heart, in order to find just the right work activities that you like. Others will give advice, but since you have to live with your choice for awhile, why not make it the one you like best out of all the others? You can change it later as you learn new skills and grow into more responsibilities you can carry out well.

Ask for My help often to clear away the doubt or confusion about all the new information and options you find. I will help you keep your focus on your heart's desires and what is best for you, if you ask Me.

If you encounter a time when nothing seems to be moving forward, call on Me for patience and help to open new avenues to explore and think about. A viable career can only be found by placing importance on what is compatible with your heart. This is the only way to determine what work path is right for you and your life. Seek to make your heart right with God first. Place My Light around yourself in quiet contemplation of what interest or area speaks to your heart, then find more information about it or people working in that area to talk with. I will be with you whenever you ask for My help.

I am Archangel Sarah

Dearest one, I am Archangel Pariti. My Light is rose pink. My purpose is to love humans who aren't able to love themselves. I send My Light to surround them in the rose color of God's love, so their heart will receive the love they need.

Many humans have so much grief and guilt, they are not able to self-appreciate all their good qualities and deeds they do for others as worthy of anyone's love. My love surrounding them dissolves all negative feelings controlling their self beliefs. Once these are all dissolved, God's love can continue to bless them every moment.

There are other negative feelings one can have to the point of saturating their energetic field around their body. If you or others you know are experiencing prolonged distress, ask for My presence and assistance. I will instantly clear and surround your body with the all powerful, all encompassing love of God. His love, continually acknowledged, praised and asked for repeatedly will heal your emotional cares and will help you believe you are worthy of His love. Once you believe with all your heart this is the truth about who you really are, you will be able to love yourself and accept love from others.

During a quiet time by yourself, ask Me to come and surround you with My loving Light from God. As the Light of God enfolds you know that self acceptance is completely possible for you. With God's Light and love all blessings are possible, if you have faith continuously in the power of God. Feel your heart gently opening to accept God's love as real. Feel the warmth and peace from the love God is surrounding you with as you imagine a beautiful pink rose or sunset.

I am Archangel Pariti

Dear ones, I am Angel Bartalamew. My Light orb is yellow as the color of a canary bird. My purpose is to assist humans who are seeking to know more about God. As My Light surrounds them when requested to do so, their minds will be cleared. I help them to understand the complexities of the infinite God. My Light opens pathways for them to learn even more about God. Since humans have come to experience and learn in a dualistic world for a time, it is sometimes hard to grasp the idea of God's ability to be everywhere at once, to be all loving to everyone on the planet and to be all knowing and all wise.

When you are seeking to know more about God ask for My assistance. My Light will come into your mind: first to clear old thoughts and beliefs that no longer serve you, so I can enlighten and inspire you with new concepts to bring new understanding of God to your thinking. I offer new abilities that will expand your mind, so you will be able to think outside of the dualistic, limited thinking you did before. God is more than you ever thought possible.

Invite Me to come and assist your reading, studying and meditations about God. I will be joyful with the opportunity to assist you in your important desire to know God intimately in your mind and heart. Think of the cheerful yellow canary singing his song of joy in the morning for another day to love God. Put God cheerfully first in your life by seeking to understand and know Him better and eventually your heart will be filled with joy.

I am Angel Bartalamew

Dearest ones, I am Archangel Omuel. My orb of Light is pink in color. My purpose is to assist humans in loving their children. Often parents choose to have children for the wrong reasons. The parents are looking to receive love and are not yet prepared to give all the love children need to grow. The human body's heart requires the love of parents. Without parental love, the child may become sickly. My loving pink Light from God will increase the ability of the parents to love their children.

My Light surrounds the heart in need of love to comfort and nourish it back to health, so the child can grow and complete its mission on earth. Once acknowledged and called for any child, My Light surrounds them and stays with them. As an Angel, I can minister to an unlimited number of children with My Light and love to nourish them. My Light will stay continuously for any children you request to have My help.

Think of any children you know or all the children in a school nearby where you live that could be held in My Light from God to help them develop and grow as God has planned for them. Call My name, acknowledge My presence with you and then ask for My Light to flash to all the children you know, know of or that come to your mind and I will instantly surround them with My pink Light of God's love. If you are willing, also think of the children in hospitals, orphanages and adoption homes, so My Light is able to help all of the children at your request. I will be grateful to you for giving Me permission to help so many deserving and wonderful creations of God's life on earth.

I am Archangel Omuel

Dearest one, I am Archangel Cammuel. My Light orb is blue like the sea. My purpose is to assist humanity with their need to give attention to their free will. Mankind does not realize that their free will is a gift from God to be used wisely and only for doing good things for others. Instead, mankind uses their free will to do whatever they think of without thought of the consequences. Much harm is created in this way.

My Light fills their minds with the Light of God's wisdom and enlightens their thinking to be able to consider what is best for all concerned in any action they might take. With purposeful and thoughtful action, no one is harmed unnecessarily. Changing ones thinking will change one's life for the better.

I come to give wisdom and enlightenment to anyone who is ready to be responsible in their life choices. Many humans have not had a parent, other family members and adults to teach them to be wise, responsible and to consider one's actions before doing them.

Call My name, Archangel Cammuel and ask for My presence with you. Acknowledge My ability to assist your thinking and decision making and I will place My blue Light in your mind. Relax and think about God and what He would want you to do. If you choose to be thoughtful and responsible in your actions towards others, your life will be a helpful blessing for other's lives. You can learn to be responsible, wiser in your choices and bring more good into the world which will ultimately bless you.

I am Archangel Cammuel

To all, I am Archangel Cefelia. My Light orb is shimmering white with fuchsia edges. My purpose is to help humankind to believe that God exists in their hearts. Many humans believe that God exists in heaven to judge them by their mistakes. The truth is God lives in their heart, with only love for everyone.

Oftentimes, mankind feels God is distant from them, when the reality is He is always right there beating their hearts. His presence within and His love are the very life of everyone. That is why your body is a temple of God. He has abided in this temple before you were born. The first heartbeat is a sign of His presence with you throughout life.

It is God's desire that you live your life knowing for certain that He is with you in a loving and close way, as no other. Acknowledging His closeness and care, you create a connection of hearts. This allows all of the blessings and love from Him to enter your heart.

Doing this as often as you choose will create a path of blessings that will fill your life with joy, peace and wisdom to direct your life in constructive ways. Think of My name, Archangel Cefelia and request My shimmering white and fuchsia orb which will surround your heart. The Light will continue as you accept the blessings from God in your heart. These blessings are God's perfect love for you. Ask for My help often to continue to keep your connection with God. The blessings from this connection are immeasurable in its effect on your life.

I am Archangel Cefelia

Greetings, I am Archangel Thomas. My Light is green. Surrounding My green orb is the color of light blue. My purpose is to heal those with unexpressed emotions. My Light surrounds areas of their body and energetic field which they are not attending to in their energetic aura and body. By holding an area of negativity in healing and protective Light, I keep it from harming the human until such a time they are able to address the negativity they have stored in their aura because they could not face the problem safely by themselves. Often the traumatic reactions are too overwhelming.

Often human experience traumas and they are unable to cope with all the pain and emotions generated by the trauma. So, they bury the outcome and responses, so as not to feel it. This buried pain will eventually cause severe illness or disease they were not meant to experience. That is when I come to hold and protect. My Light will heal the pain and traumatic responses they have refused to release because of fear. Their fear which may be too much to bear keeps them locked in a potentially harmful state.

If they choose to release the fear and pain, I can assist them. By acknowledging an Angel's ability to help them, We are then given their free will permission to serve their needs. In releasing feelings one is more at peace with their emotions clear and focused on the present.

When you are ready to release old fears, injuries and pain, ask for My assistance. I am always available to answer your request for My help. Ask Me to surround you with My healing emerald green Light and protect you while you remember, feel and release your emotional pain. My protection will prevent any further harm coming to you as long as you need Me to.

I am Archangel Thomas

Dearest one, I am Angel Serafisa. My Light orb is a pearlescent white with a soft blue outer covering. My purpose is to help humanity believe in their hearts that the will of God for them is only love and acceptance of their divinity within.

Mankind has been taught through the centuries that they are failing to please an angry and judgmental god. That is not the truth. In reality, God is love, nothing else. Love is not angry, does not judge or ever punish. God loves and protects the divine, perfect being in Spirit that you really are as He created you.

This is not to say that you are freely allowed to do any harm to yourself or others as doing harm to anyone is against the Law of God. Therefore, you will have to atone for any wrongdoing that you have created. By returning what was harmed to its original perfect state, through future lifetimes, the harm done will be atoned for and corrected. In this natural way, you have judged yourself and actions and chose to come again to earth to make the corrections yourself.

Therefore, if God is not judging you, but only giving you omnipotent love, why continue to waste your God given energy feeling guilty or ashamed? You can ask God for forgiveness and put Him first in your heart by calling on Me. God's Light will cleanse your heart, mind and feelings of all negativity, so the wondrous love and blessings God has always had for you may enter and change your belief. God only wants you to know and believe that He loves you and holds you in His perfection. Call My name and ask for My Light to surround your heart, mind and feelings. Think of My white Light surrounding you in God's love, always providing you with all you need to live and stay in gratitude for this blessing always. Call on Me often and I will always come with God's love for you.

I am Angel Serafisa

Blessings from the Angels of love, My name is Archangel Theresa. My Light orb is white. My purpose is to help mankind learn the way of love from God. To all they interact with everyday love should be the basis of their thoughts, feelings and actions no matter the circumstance. In doing so, they bless the world around them and all who are sharing or touching their life in some way.

Often people in a rush or in their head just thinking, treat others as robots there to serve them or they just want them to get out of their way. In treating others with distain and thoughtlessness, the reality is they are separating themselves from God's blessings and causing harm to themselves and others. This is against God's laws. One cannot do this without atonement for the harm done. This means calling for forgiveness is the next action required. Now ask for the Angels to come and change the wrongdoing and the unseen consequences created by such irresponsible behavior to God's creation.

Others who behave in this way to you require God's love be given to them. Through your blessing them at that moment, they will be given an opportunity to learn and grow on how to behave better through your modeling the way of love for them. This act of kindness blesses you and them, so each will benefit.

Acknowledge My presence and I am there with you. Ask for My help to show you how to live the way of love and I will purify and bless you. Sit quietly and feel My white Light surround you until you have a sense of peace and love in your heart. With God's love in your heart, you are more able to love others. Call on Me when you feel the need for more of God's love and I will be there instantly.

I am Archangel Theresa

Beloved mankind, I am an Archangel of the seraphim and My name is Maruel. My Light orb is pink. My purpose, given to Me by God, the Holy of Holies is to love humanity when their grace has fallen. I am to love them until their grace has been returned. God always loves them, but humans can separate themselves from God. Grace means to be in constant connection with God.

Often humans choose to ignore God: to keep Him out of their hearts and go against His laws. In this state, God's blessings and love cannot reach them every moment, as blessings do when they are in God's grace.

Truthfully, most of humanity lives in this way. Each day is filled for work, parenting, errands and paying their bills. They may be living an honest and good life, yet they have not brought God into their hearts to reign supreme overall else. This is not to ignore the responsibilities of living. It is to seek God in your heart first and ask Him into all of the rest of your life and activities, so He may bless you with what you need to do or be, in order to live a godly life. Walking with God at your side only makes life more blessed.

I ask you to call on Me, Archangel Maruel. I will restore your grace with God, if you ask for God's forgiveness and if you make God be first in your life. My love from God, at your request removes the energetic veil of separation from around your heart, so you may receive all the blessings that have been waiting for you. The Angels that have held God's blessings for you are the beloved of God. He wants you to have all of His love and blessings.

I am Archangel Maruel

Beloved one, I am Archangel Drusmen. My Light orb is light blue. My purpose is to help mankind learn to serve others. My Light clears out egotistic and selfish desires within the hearts and minds of humanity. My Light purifies this negative energy to allow the heart and higher self the opportunity to express altruistic feelings and actions toward others and on others' behalf. This is the natural way of relating and treating others.

The world mankind lives in is the opposite, with most seeking only to serve themselves, their needs and desires first before others. One cannot spiritually grow living in this way. One has to become aware of others' needs and focus most of their time on helping others have better lives.

Presently, mankind is troubled, seeking all the wrong things, in order to feel safe and okay. Seeking outside of oneself leads only to disappointment. One can only feel truly protected and completely loved by seeking and putting God first. Anything else will never fill the emptiness of feeling is this all there is in life? What is the point? What is my purpose for living? These are just a few of the examples of the hopelessness We Angels see in the hearts and minds of humans who are so busy getting nowhere close to finding the love of God. That is because they are looking to the things of the world to give them meaning and it is never there.

Please call on Me when you are feeling hopeless and empty. I will purify and bless you immediately with God's all encompassing love. Rest quietly, thinking about how much love omnipresent and omnipotent love really is. As you do so, God's love will connect with your heart and mind. Send your love from your heart to God with your gratitude for all He is doing for you right now and for all eternity.

I am Archangel Drusmen joyful to bring you God's love every time you request My presence to be with you

With love to all humanity, I am Archangel Thadismun. My orb of Light is fuchsia. My purpose is to love mankind in ways that will bring their awareness higher in order to feel the presence of the creator within them. This presence is God's Light. Its function is to direct God's Light and love into their hearts, minds and bodies. The presence is the living God above you. Blessing you and loving you with each of your heartbeats and each breath you take. God's presence is your very life, eternally in communion with the supreme God.

Your higher body seeks your awareness and wants you to know in your heart the true reality of who you really are for eternity with God. In truth, you are a splendid being of Light more wondrous than you ever imagined: perfect, powerful, wise and loving beyond any Angels. You are truly the daughters and sons of God, the father of unfathomable creation. By understanding who you really are, you can consciously accept your birthright. Your individualized birthright is your key to the kingdom of God. This key entitles everyone to open the crystal door of God's purpose and divine plan created expressly for them at the instant God created their specific life stream. Each key and crystal door are uniquely designed for each one of humankind. No two crystal doors or keys are ever alike, as are the snowflakes.

Call My name, Archangel Thadismun and I will instantly come. Make your request for My fuchsia Light to bless your heart and mind with the awareness and feeling of your blessed higher body. Hold your hands open to receive your key and birthright and I will deliver them to you. They will be permanently etched on the energetic etheric body and all the layers of your aura, including your Soul. Forevermore, you will never leave the kingdom of God to experience the physical octave again, unless you choose of your own free will. You will forever be free of re-embodiment, if you so choose. Praise your higher self for leading and loving you to receive this most auspicious event of gaining your eternal freedom from the reincarnation of atonement in which you repaid your debts to others.

I am Archangel Thadismun

Dear ones, I am Archangel Samuel. My Light is blue. My purpose, given to Me by God, is to bless all of mankind in their search for God. I help them search their hearts for their deeper truths, in order to determine what is right for them and what is God's divine pattern set for them at their creation.

People are confused now by hearing one thing and the next moment hearing the opposite. Most of what one hears is touted as fact. In reality, none of it is near to the truth. As a result, people are becoming increasingly cynical, which is not good. Still others are puzzled about how to find out what is true in all they see and hear.

My blue Light is from the First Ray of God's Light which is focused on the will of God. As this Light penetrates your mind, the cobwebs, so-to-speak, the confusion and cynicism are purified, so your mind is clear and free of negative energies. Now you can use your mind and heart to know what is right for you and what sounds truthful or not. My Light also helps you develop your discernment which keeps you on guard for dishonesty.

When you are ready to sit quietly for a time, do so and call My name, Archangel Samuel. Then, request what you would like My help with: concentration, volition, purpose or focus. These components are shown to be of assistance to you in knowing God's will. Rest for awhile, until your mind and thinking feel clear and refreshed. I will come as often as you think of My name.

I am Archangel Samuel

I am Archangel David. My Light orb is yellow. My purpose is to bless mankind with the wisdom of God. Mankind is aware of God's wisdom; however, they are equally unaware that God's wisdom is available to them to acknowledge, request and use for the betterment of their lives or the lives of others. Humanity tumbles on their way through life without the discernment and knowledge of a wiser choice they could have made.

My yellow Light concentrates in the area of the mind to enlighten and inspire their thinking. Anytime you have a problem to solve or a challenge to meet, acknowledging My Light and calling My name will bring My Light into the physical octave where you reside. By calling on Me and asking for My help you have given your free will permission for Me to bring My Light of God to you.

In doing so, My presence is with you to answer your request for My assistance with the specific problem or challenge you are facing. Upon entering into your presence, My Light will encircle your mind to clear it completely of all superfluous solutions. My Light will also allow you to be able to approach your problem or challenge with new perspectives and inspirations. The new ideas that are possible for you to have will help you to plan a new strategy to overcome your challenges. I will remain with you until you have a positive idea or outlook on the solution. My Light is always available whenever you call.

I am Archangel David

Dearest one, I am Archangel Jarius. My Light is white with soft pink on the outside of My orb. My purpose is to purify and love everyone who is seeking to praise God with all their heart. My shimmering Light will surround their minds to connect them with one another so their love, adoration, praise, and joy will reach the heavens.

Mankind takes for granted that God is always there for them. That is why I am here. I help them realize they need to ask Me to purify their hearts and minds so they will remember to express their gratitude, love, adoration and praise to God for all of His blessings for them each day. My Light will cleanse away the debris of the world and bring them back to the love and Light of God which is their true source of life eternal.

Call on Me in the morning as you arise to begin your day and I will bless you with God's purity. Call on Me again in the evening as you retire and I will place My Light of God's purity in your hearts and minds. I will come instantly in answer to your every call and bless you with God's love and purifying Light so your feelings will turn to praising God in all His glory.

I am Archangel Jarius, your servant

Beloved one, I am Archangel Zacarel. My Light is white. My purpose is to ground the human body as long as they reside on earth. Balance is the critical point as it is possible for humans to build more electrical energy in one or many of their chakras more than the remaining ones essentially causing an imbalance within the whole system. It is important for the proper function of all chakras that balance be maintained. If not, illness may have an opportunity to encroach upon the inner physical layer of the auraic system.

Therefore, it is wise to call on Me daily to balance your chakras so your body and whole system remain in balance. Ask for My presence to be with you as you meditate each evening before retiring and I will work during the night to balance all of your energetic system. Then, when you arise in the morning you will feel refreshed, rested and whole. As a result of complete balance, each day will flow easier as God's energetic love is also flowing through your body.

Remember also to walk barefoot on the ground whenever you can as this allows your body to discharge any static, so-to-speak or additional energy you do not need. In some similar ways your body is a living battery. It must be charged and it also must discharge energy. For example, the battery that helps your car to run must be maintained correctly to function efficiently. Please take the time each day to allow Me to do the same for your precious body of earth experience so you may live healthy and long and so you may learn more about God's infinite love for you, His finest creation.

I am Archangel Zacarel

Dear one, I am Angel Duncon. My orb is the golden color of the sunrise. My purpose is to bless mankind with the golden Light of God in the morning as they arise. I will bring the prana or golden life energy to your body. This energy has collected from the earth and its plant life during the night, in order to bless humanity at the beginning of their day. It is a joy for Me to gather God's abundant life energy and give it as a blessing to all who will receive it.

Mankind is always in a rush, waking up abruptly with an alarm clock startling their system. My blessing gives them immediate peace and God's love to begin each day in a loving way with others. When one's heart is filled with God's love and one's body is energized with God's life energy, one's entire day and evening will flow much more beautifully without stress.

Stress causes the body to repel God's love. Stress can cause heart failure, high blood pressure, high cholesterol and hair loss. Taking short periods of time to breathe deeply and relax are very beneficial. This helps the body unplug the stress switch so you can go through your day smiling.

Call on Me, Angel Duncon at the first light of the day and request My golden Light to bless you with God's prana and peace for your new day. My Light will give you energy to do all you have in mind to accomplish that day.

I am Angel Duncon

Dear one, I am Archangel Arazuel. The color of My Light orb is blue. I am directed by God to lift the Souls in mankind to heaven. In the time of their transition from the earth, other Angels help the Soul to gather a momentum of energy to rise out of the physical body. Once this is gently accomplished, I am present as the Soul rises out of the physical octave. I immediately surround the Soul in My protective blue Light and escort the Soul to heaven where other Angels await their arrival and in the case of humanity, close family members and friends also are waiting for them. Once the Soul is in their familiar surroundings being cared for and protected by the other Angels, My service is complete.

Humanity has described Me through the influences of their tremendous fear of death and the unknown. Therefore, I have been painted as a dark figure. This is not God's truth. God has created Me as a being of His Light and love consisting only of the beautiful blue Light of the will of God. His will is for every life He created to always be protected in His loving Light so there is not an instant when His creation is without His all encompassing love.

I ask you to call upon Me and My loving protective heavenly blue Light at the time of transition when I can be of loving service for your loved one. Whether it is at the moment of transition or at the moment you learn of any transition call My name, Archangel Arazuel and request My Light to well assure the Soul's safe journey to heaven will have taken place for them.

I am Archangel Arazuel

Dear beloved one, I am Archangel Um Basarri. My Light orb is blue. I am directed by God to assist mankind with the will of God in all their business affairs. My blue Light surrounds their financial resources, in order to protect them from all harm. Often mankind does not realize the dangers from the sinister force that will try to create havoc in their lives. This kind of problem is meant to cause them distress and thus, break any ongoing communion they had with God.

The first thing to do is to call on Me for My protective Light to surround and sustain all your business affairs and finances with everything related to your finances in God's Light. Next, call on Me instantly when you are first aware of a problem so my Light will be enhanced to counter any discrepancies or alterations. I will instantly correct any mistake or wrong doing related to your business affairs as long as you have faith in My ability to do so regardless of appearances.

Third, it is important to reconnect your heart and mind with the love of God and ask Him to forgive your momentary lapse into fear. Call on the violet Angels to consume and purify your discordant fear that you created. Thank them with your heart's love for Their service for you. Think of God's Light surrounding your checkbook, your financial papers, your bank and place of work, as well as the computers and phones you use to manage your financial affairs. Bring His Light and abundance into all your thoughts and feelings regarding your financial resources to bless and protect them with His love.

I am Archangel Um Basarri

Dear one, I am Archangel Somalioné. My Light orb is bright yellow. I am directed by God to assist mankind in their search for the truth of God so they can find the bible scripture that speaks to their needs. I am the Angel that highlights a certain verse that will give you encouragement or enlightenment according to your current situation. I also affect the specific page to open where the special verse or verses are located. So now you, dearest one know when this happens for you it is not your imagination or an accident. God wants you to be comforted, strengthened and your heart filled with His word so you may grow spiritually closer to Him.

When you are feeling less than perfect in any way, please pick up your bible and call My name. I am there with you immediately after you speak My name. Think of God's infinite love for you and let your bible fall open where it may. I will be there with you to know what is in your heart and the very words that will speak directly to your heart. Never be afraid again when the words of your chosen verse seem to leap out of the book. It is only My presence and God's love through Me helping you to see, know and feel this is God's personal message to your heart from His heart which is full of infinite all encompassing love for you, His child of creation.

Next time you start to study or read God's word take a moment to say My name and My presence will inspire you. You will be surprised at how fitting the highlighted words are designed just for you.

It is the intention of God to show you the truth of His words for your life at the moment to inspire and enlighten you to His supreme love for you. That is all. Nothing more than using a tool you have chosen as comfort to you in your time of need. The inspiration of God will serve you well for all your life in all you are.

I am Archangel Somalioné

Dear one, I am Archangel Hilum. My Light orb is green. I am directed by God to heal all the children, especially the children who are ill with poisoning from the effects of chemicals and pollution in the water they are being given or drinking.

Humanity does not realize the seriousness of this problem or the jeopardy all life is in with the continual pollution of the earth's water. This increasingly serious problem is affecting generally small children and those that are very sensitive or allergic to chemicals in a myriad of serious illnesses. Moreover, exacerbating the problem are the physicians who 1.) do not recognize or acknowledge water pollution as a serious problem and 2.) the physicians who are taught to dispense medications or more chemicals into the already sick bodies which are designed to heal its symptoms naturally with clean water. Thus, doctors generally do not really treat the illness.

In God's world of love and healing, the Angels of Healing have God's knowledge and therefore, know the cause of the illness and that knowledge allows Them to heal precisely what is unnatural in the child's body. All true healing taking place in today's world is done by the Angels. Doctors usually make the wrong diagnosis in cases such as these. The Angels of God never make a mistake.

I ask you for the sake of the children of the world to call My name, Archangel Hilum and request My healing green Light to envelop the children of the world for their immediate healing and release from all chemicals and pollution. With your caring concern the children will be filled with God's all encompassing love and healing Light.

I am Archangel Hilum thanking and blessing you for loving the children of earth enough to call on Me often

Greetings dear one, I am Archangel Sushienae and My Light orb is blue. I am directed by God to help humanity strengthen their bodies with the will of God's blue Light. It is always from the will of God that you are able to function with all of the energy and strength you need, especially when you are serving Him by helping others.

Most often, mankind uses their will to push their bodies beyond their comfort level which also causes more aches and pains. Even more damaging to the body is the misuse of caffeine and sugar to push the body, as well as using drugs to dull the pain which only adds more toxins to the body's organs, thus causing even more damage. It all becomes a negative cycle for the body of all kinds of toxic substances placing a greater toll on the body's strength and overall ability to be in a healthful state. For example, if you have troublesome backaches or arthritis, remember to ask Me, Archangel Sushienae to surround your discomfort or pain with the heavenly blue Light of God's will for your completely strong and healthy body.

Once you speak My name, I am with you to answer your request instantly. Please sit or rest quietly for ten minutes or so to allow Me to surround and concentrate the perfect energy of God's will for you into the areas which you have requested My help with. You can nap or read something positive; however, watching exciting, emotional or destructive television programming is not helpful to your being able to relax. Call upon me when you have time to sit quietly. Feel the Light as you think of the will of God, which is always loving filling and enfolding your body with calm, peaceful assuredness of His divine perfection and the Light of His loving will for you. I will be happy to come anytime you request My help to strengthen your body.

I am Archangel Shushienae

Dearest one, I am Archangel Percipia. My Light is pink in color. My purpose is to love all of mankind, especially when they are trying to have a baby. My love from God wraps around their hearts in a special way to attract the Soul of one who is ready to enter the physical realm of earth. My Light blesses the one coming to earth also in a special way which allows them to come in peace safely.

Many couples try to have children and because they are stressed, in ill health or negative in any way with their emotions, their combined energy does not allow them to be positive candidates to be parents. My love surrounds their minds and hearts to eradicate their negative thoughts and feelings. Then, they are calm and peaceful.

If you and your spouse are in this situation trying to have a family and it is not happening or you know of a couple in the same situation, call on Me for My help will make a difference, as I can instantly be present with whoever calls for themselves or for others.

I ask you to speak My name, Archangel Percipia and request that I surround you and your spouse or the couple you are praying for with My loving pink Light of God. I immediately wrap each person in God's love and Light. Ask for this blessing to enfold the hearts and minds of those you are praying for and keep asking for My Light until there are confident thoughts and peaceful feelings that all is well. Know deeply that God's divine plan for all Souls concerned is in His infinitely wise care and love.

I am Archangel Percipia

Dear one, I am Archangel Charuel. My Light is pink. My purpose, as directed by God is to love mankind in a special way. I hold all their dreams close in My Light so each one will be safe until they need it. My Light continues to hold their dreams until each one is manifested. Of course, this does not include nightmares or negative dreams. Only the happiest dreams and wishes for being or doing something wonderful are able to enter My Light.

Should you want to remember your dreams, just request My Light to hold your dream for you until you wake up and I can release it to you. When you want to have better or happier dreams, ask Me to assist your dreaming just before you go to sleep and I will bless you with My loving Light. If you have a child having nightmares, just request my presence to be with them through the night and My loving Light will protect them, as God's love is the most powerful of all.

Call on Me daily and I will help you have wonderful dreams. God's love only creates more goodness for everyone who asks. Try asking for My Light to surround you upon retiring for a few nights and see if your dreams don't immensely improve and you remember them more easily.

I am Archangel Charuel

Dear one, I am Archangel Melore. My Light orb is a bright yellow as is the goldfinch bird. My purpose, as directed by God is to place the wisdom of God into the minds of those in humanity who are trying to find their way home to God. My yellow Light will inspire them to search for their truth in new books and organizations, in order to explore their thinking to new beliefs, ideas and activities centered on developing their belief system.

Many people today are confused, feeling hopeless and lost without a spiritual structure or foundation. This leaves them in an ungrounded state, more subject to negative influences from the world. Without strong spiritual tenets to live by many fall into negative activities that cause them much harm. In doing so, they risk putting their spiritual development back many lifetimes. When, with a stronger belief system, they would have more easily denied the requests to participate in negative choices from their peers or others.

With My bright yellow Light enfolding their mind with the wisdom of God, they are much more likely to seek an understanding of God, His laws and how to live a better life in His world, rather than the darkness of the human world. Their choices are important when young, as they can set a life for constructive work and experiences or set up a life of self-destruction.

I ask you to call on Me, Archangel Melore and request My bright yellow Light to enfold the minds of the young with the wisdom of God. I request Archangel Melore to inspire the youth of the world to seek an understanding of God, His laws, how to live a higher life of good in this world and be strong enough to withstand the negative pressures of the world.

I am Archangel Melore thanking you for your assistance on behalf of the world's children and young adults

Precious ones, I am Archangel Butyalil and My Light orb is white in nature. My purpose is to bring the will of God to all of His natural creation, including all vegetation, inland bodies of water, rivers and streams and every elemental serving them. My action is to oversee and coordinate all of the Light beings: Angels, Powers of Nature and the Elementals all acting in God's perfect balance for the harmony of all life.

My love for all of nature is immense and God's love for His creation is exceedingly more vast and encompassing to all. I come to be with you to encourage you to seek God and His love by enjoying the magnificent beauty and majesty in all of nature. His wondrous creation of such diversity, marvel and interest are His loving examples of His love. By creating such an array of mountains, waterways, valleys and planes, deserts and rolling pastures and all the variety of vegetation inherent to all of these vistas, God is providing you especially with a wondrous view to experience, enjoy and feel His abiding love for you, His masterpiece of creation.

I lovingly invite you to do whatever you can where you reside on mother earth, to enjoy and experience for yourself or with family and friends, all the loving energy from God that is gently beckoning you to explore. Within each moment of being in nature, your Soul is blessed far more than you realize by all the wondrous and loving Light beings God has created to bring harmony, solace and joy to your heart and mind to comfort your body.

With all My love, I am Archangel Butyalil

Greetings dearest one, I am Archangel Baramion. My Light orb is fuchsia and the purpose God gave Me is to direct God's love to all mankind. Specifically, I am directed to bless the hearts and minds of humanity. It is with great joy and love I send this blessing to all who seek to serve God and to do His will even in the seeming smallest of actions and words of obedience.

Mankind is often taught they are sinners and therefore, are unworthy of God's love and acceptance. This is not God's truth. He always loves and accepts the Souls He created which is all of humanity. This truth is without exception; however, that does not include the harm, negativity or discord humans choose to create. God's omnipotent perfection will not accept or recognize anything less than the perfection in which He created all and which He holds every Soul within.

With God's love and acceptance comes His complete forgiveness for any wrong done or mistakenly created. Therefore, His loving arms, so-to-speak, are ever open waiting for the moment you ask for His forgiveness. Then, the blessings from God that have been held for you flow again freely to help you in the very way you need most. So, ask for His forgiveness and give Him your love and gratitude for blessing you as a kind and wise father loves his child. For those who request My help, I will bring to you all of God's blessings in an instant, as soon as you ask Me to.

I am forever joyfully in your service, Archangel Baramion

Dear one, I am Angel Timothy. My Light is the color of love: soft pink. My purpose is to love humanity in the special way of giving unconditional acceptance. I surround and fill the hearts of mankind with God's love while they are sleeping. Without God's love the human heart will stop beating. I go to those who are not receiving enough love from humans. By enfolding their hearts with God's love, they feel better and will not become depressed.

Many people live alone, are away from family or have no family on earth or choose to be solitary. There are many such situations that exist in the lives of humanity at this time, as people also choose to move away from family for employment. This leaves them in need of more love and I bring them God's love which is the best of all.

If you are in this situation or know of someone living alone permanently or for a time, you can call on Me, Angel Timothy and I will answer your call immediately. Just request God's love from Me to be brought to whomever you choose and give Me their full name, so I can carefully answer and fulfill your every request. Thank you for allowing Me to serve God by bringing His loving pink Light to those you know and think of who are in need of His wondrous love.

I am Angel Timothy

Peace be to humanity, I am Archangel Jamal. My orb Light is violet. The purpose given to Me by God to perform for mankind is the raising of the Soul at the ascension in the glory of God for all humanity. God's violet Light is the most powerful purifier of humanity's discordant energy created by each one as they serve themselves above serving God, the great creator of all life.

When you choose to serve the flesh in anyway, no matter how small it seems, you are placing God in second place and putting your body and its desires above Him, the Holy of Holies in all of creation. In order to serve God first and seek Him and His righteousness or right living first, you must place all desires of the body as insignificant and not worthy of any transgression against God's will.

This is not to declare that the body should not be revered as the holy temple of God. It is your task with each choice to place the crown of God's will upon God as king in your living temple of God. With God in His rightful place as Lord Most High of all you are, His blessings flow abundantly to you and your body. However, placing Him second will cause His blessings to be held by the Angels until you awake to your wrong doing, ask for His forgiveness and then, keep Him first in your life with every choice.

Call on My name, Archangel Jamal and ask for the purifying violet Light of God and His forgiveness. I will see that all of your discord is transmuted into God's perfect Light.

I am at your service as Archangel Jamal

Felicitations, I am Archangel Pahuel. My Light is green. I am directed by God to heal all mankind of their physical aches and pains. My purpose is to help all of mankind to experience the peace and love of God's comforting Light. My Light is directed to enfold any area within one's body that is feeling uncomfortable so that area will relax and gently return to its normal state.

With mankind's present life their bodies are experiencing a great deal of stress and strain which causes the body to tense up muscles. In time this tenseness will cause muscles to fill with toxins making them sore. Stress also causes blood vessels to constrict lowering circulation which makes it more difficult for the muscles to release the toxins and relax. Even children are experiencing tension and stress to do well in school, avoid being bullied or ridiculed and all sorts of other possible stressors. It is important to keep the physical body healthy with adequate water, healthy food and exercise. It is also equally important to keep the body in its natural state, not in a fearful state which stress creates.

I encourage you to call to Me, Archangel Pahuel to request My healing green Light from God to surround your entire body with His peace and love until you feel physically comforted and calm. I will immediately answer your call and enfold you in God's comforting and healing green Light until you feel rested, refreshed and without any aches or tension. It is also good to call Me just before you retire and do the same for your children's health and well being.

With peace, I am Archangel Pahuel

Serving all is My joy, I am Archangel Thadimus. My Light is yellow and with it I bless the minds of mankind with God's wisdom as He has directed Me to do. God's wisdom is needed greatly by mankind at present so they know what is best for them from God, instead of what the world directs them to do.

Mankind, without God's wisdom is easily swayed by the sinister force to follow the wrong people, do and say discordant things and thus, create many more problems for themselves and others. It is God's wisdom that directs mankind away from creating discord. None other will do this for you. He is the only One leading mankind who will heed His wisdom into heaven.

God's wisdom will teach you, show you the way and bring you into perfection. He wants only all that is best for you, nothing else.

If you wish to receive God's wisdom call My name Archangel Thadimus and request My yellow Light to enfold and surround your brain and mind so that God's wisdom will direct you in the perfect way He would have you go in every choice you make, words you speak and actions you take which will bring you to heaven with Him for eternity.

Archangel Thadimus

Dearest one, I am Archangel Purci. My Light is fuchsia pink, with a violet center. My Light is God's purifying love brought from heaven to bless mankind. I fill their hearts with purifying love so their heart is cleansed of all wrong feelings towards others. When this is completed their heart center is open to receive all of God's wonderful love. The effect this has on humans allows them to feel God's love.

Mankind may know in some respect that God loves them; yet, it is only a thought or belief. Yes, God wants you to know He loves you and all of His creation; however, it is still more important that one actually feels within their heart God's love. When this is accomplished deep within one's feelings, God increases His blessings. With this deeper connection, God will bring all of His wisdom, truth, peace, will and great love to you in every way. There is only one way to receive all of His love and blessings and that is with a pure and open heart filled with all of your love for Him.

If you will call My name, Archangel Purci and request My fuchsia pink and violet Light to enter your heart center, I will purify your heart and fill your heart to overflowing with immense love for your creator. Ask Me to come to you every day with God's purifying love so you may receive all of His wondrous blessings the Angels have been holding just for you. Never doubt that His love, wisdom, truth, beauty and peace are the will of God for you, His blessed child of the Light. Open your heart and receive all the purifying love of God and its power. With this perfect love, transforming your life is possible by the power of God's love.

I am Archangel Purci sent by God

Blessings to all, I am Archangel Ongkanon. My orb is golden. I am directed by God to send My Light to every human being that is trying to communicate the love of God to mankind. My Light envelopes the human mind with God's all powerful golden Light of God's wisdom. In doing so, their mind is enlightened with God's knowledge.

God's knowledge will assist the one who is offering their service for the good of all mankind in that it blesses them for serving others, instead of serving themselves. This is His will for those that serve Him first above all else. Also, God's knowledge will lead His servant to where they should go. His wisdom will tell them who they should see to share their service with. God's knowledge will teach His servant the Mysteries of Life Eternal and will bring the servant to the Light they serve.

God is wanting His servants to understand the truth of their beings in Him is perfection, beauty and love eternal. God, the Father only knows His servant's perfection in His Light. He does not recognize the finite embodiment. God only knows His true servants as the perfect beings He created.

I ask you to call on Me, Archangel Ongkanon and request the golden Light of God's wisdom to assist you in every way possible in your service to mankind so that mankind will be blessed greatly by every effort you are making to help humanity know God's truth, will and love. When you call Me I will surround your mind, heart and body with the golden Light of God so He may bless you greatly with all you need to continue to serve His Light. You will know His presence by seeing and feeling His golden Light enfolding you.

I am Archangel Ongkanon

Dear one, I am Archangel Charity. My Light orb is white. My purpose is to direct the white Light of God to all mankind that are hoping to find the truth of God in their lives. My white Light will show them the way by enlightening their minds with God's truth and Light. I am able to pierce all doubts, confusion and old beliefs out of their mental field and replace them with confidence, clarity and an openness to find and accept the truth from God.

Mankind is often closed and bound in by outgrown tenets and beliefs. These mind constructs become limiting and keep one from receiving inspiration and new ideas to move forward in their lives. My white Light from God is designed with God's love to free all humanity from anything that attempts to hold mankind from reaching upward to the Light of God.

It is important for mankind to evolve spiritually, ever placing the Light of God as their supreme goal for their life. Seeking God's Light is vital to becoming His servant and attaining eternal life.

Speak these words: I call to Archangel Charity. I request Archangel Charity to answer my hope to find the truth of God for my life by directing the white Light of God to enlighten my mind with God's truth and Light, filling me with God's confidence in my discernment, God's clarity in my decision making and giving me openness to find and accept the truth of God for my life.

I am Archangel Charity hoping you will call for My Light often

Beloved one, I am Archangel Chamuel. My Light orb is fuchsia. My purpose is to direct the loving Light of God to mankind's hearts so they may feel the love God has for them, His wonderful creation.

I ask you to feel for a moment the greatest love you have felt in your lifetime. Take your time remembering. When you have determined the exact memory, hold it is your mind's eye for as long as you like. See every detail that you can clearly. Remember how you felt in that moment.

Could you feel your heart opening with love? Did you feel your lips smiling? Did you eyes well up with tears of happiness? Remember your loving memory again to check for any physical reactions you may have had. Are there others you felt?

Now, with the memory of your greatest moment of feeling love, allow Me to assure you God's love for you just as you are reading this page right now is infinitely more. Take your feelings of love from your memory and expand it from your heart to fill all infinite space. This is how much God loves you. Can you even imagine this much love?

Call My name. Request My fuchsia Light to enter your heart. God's love instantaneously surrounds you completely with His love. Send your love up to Him with your praise and gratitude. Become an empty vessel and allow His love to completely fill you to overflowing with His magnificent love for you.

I am Archangel Chamuel

Beloved, My name is Archangel Christine and My Light is white. I am the Twin Flame of Archangel Jophiel. We balance the Light of God for mankind in the area of love and purity. My contribution is to bring the white Light of God to each one's need for purity in their hearts.

God's purifying Light will remove all unnatural guards, walls and barriers placed within the heart center by each individual for self-protection in response to their experiencing great harm, trauma or pain caused by another person mistreating them. Often the individual does not realize their heart center contains these negative, self-made emotional barriers, self-created unconsciously by the ego in the human personality. It is simply a self-defense mechanism; however, these barriers prevent the individual from being completely emotionally free. These barriers or walls around the heart center may also be carried into one's current life on earth from previous lifetimes in which trauma, extreme hardship or painful illnesses were experienced.

If you choose to have all of these barriers removed, say out loud: I call Archangel Christine. I request the purifying white Light of God be brought to my heart center by Archangel Christine to surround my heart center. Purify and remove all barriers, walls and self-defenses there from all of my embodiments upon earth and anywhere else in God's universes according to God's law, love and Light of perfection for His creation. I accept and feel in my heart center the purifying white Light of God in one mighty flash setting my heart free! I am God's perfect being in God's purifying Light.

I am Archangel Christine at your service as God commanded Me to be for you forever

Beloved one, I am Archangel Moroni. My white Light is directed by God to bring the pure enlightenment of God's mind, love, wisdom and peace to all mankind who are earnestly seeking to do His will, lovingly praying to Him and wanting with all their hearts to serve Him above all else.

I want you to know the Angelic Host is waiting and watching for every call to Them so They may bring all of God's blessings to those that call. It is the greatest joy for the Angels to bless humanity with God's blessings for everyone.

In reading this, you have acknowledged all Angels in the universes of God as magnificent Beings of God's love, Light, purity, joy and service to all life. Your acknowledgement in this important way gives permission to the Angelic Host to be in the physical octave. This creates a tremendous outpouring of God's love to all life on earth. Your seeking to know and call the Angels is a far greater blessing than you realize, as you are helping to change the world. It will become a world of peace, health, prosperity, one community sharing with and serving others, perfect weather, pure water, abundant food and all living and experiencing God's perfect creation once again. This is all because you are choosing to acknowledge God and His Angels every day. I hope you will continue to call knowing in your heart you have allowed all these wondrous Beings to create the final golden age of God for all humanity, the animals and the earth in infinite space.

It will be My joy to instantly answer your every call. Call to Me as Archangel Moroni and request My white Light to enlighten your mind with the knowledge, wisdom, love and will of God for your life. I will flash My Light to enfold you with the triune of a balanced life from God so you will live a balanced life. I will be with you as long as you hold the peace and love of God in your heart. With this blessing you will continue to advance your Soul higher in God's sight.

I am Archangel Moroni serving you in God's love and Light forever.

Blessed one, I am Archangel Martin. My Light is white and I am directed by God to send His white Light to all of mankind to flash purifying Light to their minds, hearts and bodies. God desires all of mankind to be enlightened, to have loving hearts and to have bodies that are pure. I am directed to assist any human who is seeking God first in their lives.

My assistance consists of flashing God's white Light through their body, especially their heart and mind to purify and remove all energies that are not pure like God's Light. I will continue to bless them until all these lesser energies have been transmuted into God-like Light again. The assistance of My directed Light will enhance the individual's ability to be inspired, their feelings will be positive and loving from a heart which is open and pure and their body will be energized with God's Light and love.

If you are seeking God in your mind, heart and actions wanting to make Him first in your life every moment, then call to Me. Speak these words while standing: I call to Archangel Martin. I request Archangel Martin to flash the purifying white Light of God throughout my body, especially my mind and heart. I request Archangel Martin to purify and remove all energies that are not pure like God's Light. I ask Archangel Martin to continue to bless me until all these lesser energies are transmuted into God-like Light again. That is completely what you need to speak every day to become a vessel of God filled with His pure Light and love.

I am Archangel Martin waiting for your calls

Dear one, I am Archangel Marion. My Light is white. My purpose is to illuminate all the hearts and minds of humanity so they will feel and know God's Light and love. I enfold them with the dazzling white Light from God and it purifies them instantly of all negative feelings, thoughts and beliefs or attitudes that no longer serve their highest good.

Change is sometimes very difficult for some to embrace and see the good it will bring. They focus on what they think and feel they are losing in changing, instead of all the wonderful new things and ways of living better that are all just waiting for them.

Other people face change as a part of life; that life on earth is temporary and so is everything else. With this viewpoint they are able to accept change much more easily. Whereas the first groups' viewpoint is that it is important to avoid change. Keeping the status quo gives them a false feeling of security. The only way to get out of one's resistance to change is to ask yourself: what are you afraid of? Is it losing everything or is it that the new is unknown and therefore, fearful? Fear is at the root of any consternation regarding changing one's life in any way.

I can help, if you acknowledge My by name and request My white Light to come to you or someone you know instantly. I will immediately surround all with the purifying white Light of God, giving God's love and cleansing of all negative energy. By accepting God's purification and assistance to eradicate all negative feelings, thoughts and beliefs, one will feel free to move forward, accept change and see its inherent goodness from God.

I am Archangel Marion

Salutations, I am Archangel Mallory. My Light orb is white and My purpose is to enlighten the minds of mankind with the truth of God's wisdom, will and love. Anyone who is seeking to know God and the ancient truths of the ages, as well as His loving will for their lives may call upon Me for My assistance and instruction.

I teach the knowledge of long ago and now forgotten civilizations that have been lost to present day history of mankind. I will instruct every willing and dedicated student of truth in the ways of the ancient sages, as well as the ancient truth sayers who passed the wise knowledge verbally down through the generations for tens of thousands of earth years.

I have been with the sages and truth sayers from the beginning of mankind's time and I have been with God before man's time began. Every civilization has wise ones who gather and glean the truths of the Soul, the eternal Supreme Creator and the way to perfection.

It is My hope that you are seeking to learn the truth about God and want to find out for yourself what your truth is for this lifetime and your Soul. I would ask you to call upon Me before your evening retiring with these spoken words: I call to Archangel Mallory. I request your white Light of the will of God to envelope my mind with the great mysteries of ancient knowledge. I ask Archangel Mallory to teach me what I need to know to be able to follow God's will for me completely. With this request made every night just before you sleep, I have your permission to instruct you in the ways of the wise ones from long ago.

I am Archangel Mallory awaiting your call

Dearest one, I am Archangel Sicily. My Light is white and My purpose is to purify mankind's hearts and minds of all habits and cravings that are not for their highest good. My Light purifies their minds and hearts of all old and no longer useful beliefs, habits and fears which cause cravings in their physical bodies. In doing so, old habits and cravings are easily released. By releasing energies which no longer serve you your life will be blessed.

Humanity often does not realize they are behaving out of outdated ideas, beliefs and feelings which have caused habits to form. They continue on in this way without thinking or realizing the potential negative effect this has on their overall health, happiness and well-being. It is My purpose to help them realize and change their life for the betterment of their Soul.

If you want to change old habits or release old beliefs and ideas, call on Me for My assistance. I will come to you immediately to enfold you in God's purifying white Light which will purify and release all unneeded energy that is holding you back from being able to change and move forward.

Call on Me, Archangel Sicily to request the white Light of God to purify your mind, heart and body of all unneeded ideas, beliefs, feelings, habits and cravings. I will instantly surround you with God's pure white Light continuously until you are completely free from all obsolete energies that have been stored within your aura for too long.

I am Archangel Sicily

Beloved one, I am Archangel Timothy. My Light is yellow. I am directed by God to bless the minds of mankind with God's wisdom. My Light enfolds each one's thoughts and beliefs with the Light of God, in order to bless each one with God's wisdom so they can live better lives. God's yellow and golden Light of wisdom clears one's thoughts and beliefs of all that is of no longer use, due to spiritual growth and changes through living and learning.

Mankind often holds on to old beliefs and forgets or does not know thoughts create energies that will remain in their auras or energetic patterns. It is important and very helpful to ask for these unused ideas, old thoughts and beliefs to be cleansed allowing for clear thinking and reasoning to function naturally in one's mind.

I ask you to call on Me verbally as Archangel Timothy. Request that I bring the golden and yellow Light of God's wisdom to your mind to cleanse away all negativity and outdated thoughts, ideas and beliefs to help your mind be refreshed, renewed and clear. I will come instantly upon your call with the Light of God's wisdom to cleanse and teach you the marvelous truths and wisdom of God.

I am Archangel Timothy

Dearest one,

I am Archangel Aragon. My Light is white. I am directed by God to flash His white Light of purification to all humanity who is seeking the way of God on earth. God's blazing white Light will purify anyone who asks for His assistance.

The world of mankind is so filled with darkness and negativity that it can be overwhelming to those who are unaware of its cause. It is easy to be lulled into thinking this is just the way life is; however, it is not. In truth, God designed life to be full of Light and all things good for the development of mankind's Souls. It is God's desire to have all of mankind living in abundance, health and peace.

Until all mankind is purified by God's white Light, you can call on Me, Archangel Aragon to bring the purifying white Light of God to bless you, those you know and love or those in great need around the world. Ask Me, Archangel Aragon to flash God's all powerful, purifying white Light into the physical octave continuously and I will instantly be with you to answer your call in every way.

I am most grateful for your calls and will immediately bring God's white Light to purify whomever or wherever you ask Me. In doing so, it is My heartfelt joy to serve God by bringing His perfect white Light of purification into the physical octave of mankind.

I am Archangel Aragon

Blessed ones, I am Archangel Tifany. My Light orb is violet. My purpose is to purify all negative human discord created among families who are joined with the marriage vows of their children.

Often in human experiences, marriages create discord among each family concerned which builds over time at the marriage continues, separates or divorce dissolves the marriage and relationships. For whatever reason perceived to be an inequity or injustice much discord is created in this kind of situation around all that are within the two families. The discord surrounding all only creates even more animosity and misunderstanding which creates even more discord for all concerned. The only way to purify all discord is through the purifying violet Light of God.

If you are in a similar marital situation or know of others experiencing this discord call to Me, Archangel Tifany and request the purifying violet Light of God to surround everyone involved continuously, especially in their hearts and minds until all discord is dissolved and transmuted. The violet Light will do wonders. Call on Me often to continue to purify all discord and I will instantly enfold all concerned with God's loving and purifying Light.

I am Archangel Tifany of the Violet Angels of God's love

Beloved, I am Archangel Cephrus. My Light orb is rose pink. I am directed by God, the Holy One of all life to bless mankind with extricating the discord created by their emotions related to their beliefs and feelings of unworthiness. These beliefs and emotions create discord that gathers around their hearts, blocking out the love of God they need to survive every day. This negative energy, if left to build will eventually cause a heart attack and often an earlier death.

My pink Light releases the negative energy so the Angels of Love are able to free all of this discord and the heart is freed to function more efficiently. Since heart attacks are a major cause of death, it would be advised for everyone to ask the Angels for Our assistance. We willingly and joyfully answer every call that is made requesting Our assistance.

Begin by calling on Me, Archangel Cephrus. Request My pink Light of God to enfold your heart to release all negative energy surrounding your heart created by any and all beliefs and feelings of unworthiness. Thank God, the Holy One of all life for this life giving blessing especially brought to you. Then, your feelings of unworthiness are removed until you come home full of Light.

There you will find all waiting for you is love, only love. It is your birthright from God to have complete self-assuredness in all of your being for evermore. With all unworthiness healed, there is only peace and love.

I am Archangel Cephrus

Greetings dear one, I am Archangel Stephen. My Light orb is white and My purpose is to bless all of mankind with the white Light of God, the Supreme Being in a special way. I enfold God's Light around all of humanity's hopes and dreams to keep them safe from the sinister force.

Mankind holds their aspirations for their future lives within their heart centers. If the sinister force is able to attack this area, it will discourage or destroy these aspirations, if allowed to do so. However, with God's Light enfolding these precious aspirations, the sinister force is completely powerless to do any harm.

Please understand the aspirations are held in a slightly different area of the heart center than where God's Spark of Life beats the heart of everyone, so that area is not accessible or subject to the sinister force in any way. With the human's hopes and dreams being housed outside of the secret chamber of the heart, it is then vulnerable to the negative emotions. Therefore, great disappointments and the like open one's aspirations to attack.

My Light protects continuously, when called to do so. Speak My name. Request My Light to enfold the area of your heart holding all your dreams, hopes and aspirations for your life with God's all powerful white Light continuously. I will answer your call immediately. You can also request this blessing from God for others you know and love or wish to pray for. I am always at your service with God's loving, protective and all powerful Light.

I am Archangel Stephen

I am Archangel Mita. My Light is white. My purpose which God has given to Me is to bring the white Light of purpose to mankind giving them direction and inspiration to complete their purpose. Often mankind lose their way as they encounter the challenges of life on earth and they lose the momentum necessary to manifest their individual life purpose given to them before they came to earth. My loving task is to continue to give everyone God's Light designed to rekindle and reenergize their desire to manifest and complete their life purpose.

God's all powerful white Light consists of all the love, energy and intelligence needed by every individual to complete their specific life purpose. With God's Light and love, there is not a possibility of any kind of failure in manifesting and completely finishing their life purpose.

If you know your life purpose, then call on Me, Archangel Mita and ask Me to bring and surround all of your being with the white Light of God immediately. As you receive His blessings, fill your heart with gratitude and love to God for His Divine Plan enlivened within you this day and every day you make this request until your life purpose is completed in all its glory for mankind.

I am Archangel Mita, God's servant

Dearest, I am Archangel Jessanel. My Light orb is golden yellow. I am directed by God to assist mankind in their search for God's Light. It is imperative all humanity finally choose to seek God's Light; however, not in the world of mankind for it is not there. One must turn to one's heart and seek God's Light there.

If you are willing to let the noise and emptiness of the illusionary world you live in go and no longer give it your undivided attention, you will find a place of quiet love and strength within your heart which has been there all along waiting patiently for your attention to turn to all life, all love and all wisdom within you. The world outside of you can only disappoint and ultimately will no matter your circumstances. Due to its nature created by mankind the world of mankind can do nothing else but fail you with its inherent imperfection.

With your desire to seek God's Light first, a new world within you will open to reveal its peace, calm, love and unlimited assistance to help you grow spiritually. All you need to do is continue to seek asking for Our assistance. For instance, you are always welcome to call upon Me by name and I will be with you instantly. Ask for My assistance to seek God's Light in your heart and to have revealed gently to you all the loving plans God has designed just for your life. My white Light will enfold you in His loving will created just for you and no other. I will always come at your call.

I am Archangel Jessanel

Beloved one, I am Archangel Remliel. My Light from God is white. My purpose is to bring God's white Light to humanity who are seeking God's flame of life in their hearts with reverence. I guide them in their prayers and meditations to God's flame within.

In mankind's world you are taught to look outside of yourself for what you think you need, believing in the false power of the world to provide the resources you need to be able to live. Mankind can stay so busy in trying to accumulate these things they do not ever find the true source of all life within from which all we have comes to us from the one true source. I am here to assist those who are searching and for those who have realized there must be a simpler way to live, yet have not found the answer which has always been waiting within them.

As you sit quietly, I ask you to call Me, Archangel Remliel. Ask Me to surround your entire being with God's white Light. Think about God giving you life. Feel your heart beating with His Light and love within it. Know you are one with the great life of all life: God, the mighty of all life. Praise and thank this holy life within you continuously. God is there with you loving you as His perfect creation.

I am Archangel Remliel, with you instantly at your every call to bring you God's life energy

The Act of Decreeing

Those who are not familiar with the act of decreeing might welcome a brief explanation of the technique in giving decrees. The process of decreeing is not difficult to master, although diligence and attention to detail is needed to speak the decrees written by the Angels. It is very important to enunciate every word clearly and with heartfelt emotion speaking every word with love and the knowledge of God's presence with you. His omnipotent Light is encased in each syllable of the words the Angels have written to be spoken through the caller, in order to bring the Light of God into the plane of physical earth.

The Angels wish to deliver God's perfection to humanity. These decrees are a vehicle in which the Angels are given the green light to encompass the words spoken in God's Light, permitting Light to enter into every word forming a focus of Light into the physical world. The focal prism becomes the guide of every word now filled with Light. The words follow the focused Light's intention rushing faster than the speed of the physical sun's light to fulfill the decree. Instantly, the Angelic Host is present to hold the constructive Light within the decree until the decree's intention is perfectly completed.

For the caller, it is imperative to stand while speaking the decree chosen. By holding peace, love and complete confidence in feeling and thought, every decree is given with the assurance of the fulfillment in its entirety. By doing so, one's positive energetic imprint sets into motion upon the decree a platform of peace and love in which to launch the Light-filled words into the limitless expanse of life as God created all life to be: in a constant state of perfection. In essence, the Light-filled decree contains the Life Substance of perfection giving to the intended recipient, condition or situation mentioned in the decree, the original Light and perfection as God created. This applies to every seeming and temporary situation a decree could contain. Wherever there is life, there is always the spark of God's Life within every need which will respond instantly to the Light given with every decree. The words sent to every need and amplified by the called Angel will enfold the need with the original perfection as God created it. In recognizing and loving the spark of God's Life in all currently seen the eternal Life of Creation, as it was originally created to be has been given an immense blessing. Far beyond what can be imagined, this act of love constitutes the greatest and most true service one can give: using one's God-given life, feeling and thought to lovingly speak the words of truth filled with Light for all in desperate need.

Within the writing of every Angel is the instruction and the precise words needed to stand and speak a decree. As every Angel's name is spoken at the beginning of the decree the Angel called is instantaneously present. As the decree is spoken the Angel enfolds the caller. The life energy you are giving by speaking the decree in truth is Light. The caller's intention and permission for the decree allows the Angel to now act within the physical world as the decree directs. If the caller chooses to speak a decree or several decrees every day, Light will continue to expand and the Angel or Angels given permission by the caller's requests may continue to do more as the decree has directed.

The Angels will always love every one and respect their right to choose which decree or decrees they wish to speak. As the decrees are given, the Angels enfold the caller with God's love and blessings for their valued assistance to the Angelic Host's service to God. Consider yourself, as you speak the decrees, as an integral participant in the Angels' service to all of humanity, life and earth upon which you reside. Your service will forever bring you countless blessings and love from the Angelic Host for allowing more angelic service and blessings to enfold humanity in this way. This is the Angelic Host's joyful purpose: to serve and bless humanity and all life for eternity with love and blessings to all.

Glossary

Angelic Host: Created by God in ever unlimited numbers, the Angelic Host are the servants of the Light who in loving joy assist All Life created by God with exultation, service and love to the one God. The Angelic Host wait upon God in complete harmony, order, joy, wisdom, holiness and the exaltation of God and His omnipotent Light. The Light of God is the directive force of love for the host of Angels created by God. Their mission is to serve God and His creation with love; the most powerful, intelligent force in all of creation.

Angels of Healing: The Angelic Host also has other groupings dependent on the particular service being rendered. These services are a vast array of diverse services given for the betterment of all requesting Their assistance. Some of these services are related to healing, as well as all of the services offered within these writings. There is an unlimited amount of the Angelic Host to address and assist every humanly created problem within the physical plane.

Ascended Masters: The Ascended Host are in service to the Light of God to expand and extend It's reach into every area in which the sinister force has temporary hold upon mankind. The Ascended Ones are unfailing in Their quest to annihilate all darkness. There is no force in existence that can or will win against Them. In every instance, They are victorious in using the cosmic consciousness of all that is good, pure and Light to vanquish all deceit and discord for the ascension of all life to occur. The Ascended Masters are ever present to assist one who has risen in Light enough to warrant Their Light, life energy and love to carry them further in their personal choice to follow the Light of God over all else within the physical realm of life. They are willing to reach back in their ascension path to assist those who have farther to rise with the love and Light of God which will elevate them more than they can know at their level of existence. Searching for the Light in oneself is paramount to this process of eternal growth.

Chakras: The Vedas, the oldest written hymns in the history of India are the first known to mention this system of physical and spiritual energy centers. The word chakra is from Sanskrit terminology meaning wheel of light. The chakra system is believed to be the regulatory foundation of energy management within and without the body, including the physical, emotional, mental and spiritual levels. These energetic centers, beginning below the feet and progressing up the body to over several feet above the head, are an open system and function as connection points in which energy is constantly rotating and flowing as the chakras respond and receive outer and inner stimulus.

Chohan: An ascended master who has risen in further attainment to be designate in charge of one of the Rays of Light which are focused spiritual energy or Light emanating from Infinite Source.

Cosmic Beings: These are the celestial beings of great wisdom Light and love for the planet earth, humanity and all life upon the planet. They have come from distant and near planets within the universes of God's creation to serve the Light, in order to save earth, assist in its ascension, as well as the ascension of mankind into the final Golden Age of Eternity. They are great Beings of immense Light, wisdom and power which emit a celestial energy which holds the planet of earth in balance, as it currently is constantly effected by all of the tremendous lower energy created by humanity with its wars, destruction and chaos. Without these Cosmic Beings, the earth would not be able to sustain its orbit correctly and it is this tremendous imbalance of energy that is causing the earth to dissipate this imbalance with earthquakes and more extreme weather. Humanity owes a great debt of gratitude to the Cosmic Beings who are helping tremendously to maintain the equilibrium of earth until mankind realizes its waywardness and misuse of earth is the sole cause of the extreme physical conditions and weather related to destruction upon earth.

Discord: This word signifies all of the various negative results of humanity's choices, either in ignorance or disobedience to allow their physical body, emotions, thoughts and beliefs misguide them instead of placing the Almighty God on the altar place reigning supreme in the direction of all areas of their lives while on earth. It is this one paramount choice to be made in all things which will create harmony in one's experience by placing God first in one's life or create chaos, if one chooses to place the world of the physical realm before the One Supreme Being of All Life.

Earth's ascension: Earth is a living being created by the Supreme Being of All Life as a perfect orb of Light for man. Earth's ascension is the process of this planet returning to this original perfection. As the great teacher Jesus Christ has taught and demonstrated unequivocally, the ascension of mankind is possible. For earth to make her complete ascension, man must also ascend. The one depends upon the other. As mankind raises itself by following God's higher direction in all things peace, love, harmony and praise to the One Supreme Being creates perfection. Then, earth will begin its physical rise into the Light. In the etheric realms, the ascension has already begun and will continue without mankind's assistance. Yet, in this circumstance earth's rise will be tumultuous and difficult for mankind until, as a consensus they realize their actions are the cause of the tumult and chaos. When mankind realizes their discord is the cause of the chaos upon the earth and they turn to Light, the God of All Life in praise and love for all, the total ascension will be in place for earth to ascend to its former glory in God's Light.

Great White Brotherhood Within the ascended master's realm, the Great White Brotherhood is an order of the highest rank, dedicated to directing the Light into the darkness of the physical realm of discord. It is their charge to bring the Light to every person who is trying to find the Light, truth and wisdom to live in harmony at all times in all circumstances. Their other charge is to direct the Light to all areas besieged by the temporary dark forces on earth. With the all powerful Light of the Supreme Being, they shall not fail in eradicating all darkness, discord and destruction from planet earth.

Inner sight: The inner sight is another term for the inner eye. Both refer to a type of vision which relies on other perceptions outside of the parameters of physical sight. Inner sight is predicated upon the alignment of the pituitary gland, the sixth chakra located between and slightly above the eyebrows and the crown chakra slightly above the top of the head in the physical human body. Through the opening of these chakras and the alignment of the universal Light of life flowing into the crown chakra, once the pituitary gland is positioned correctly, the inner sight becomes open. This is a gift, if it occurs naturally on its own through the spiritual development of its recipient. The inner sight can unknowingly or knowingly be forced to open and function; however, the person is then subject to much distress with exposure to the lower energies that are within the psychic realm of human creation which is full of discord. This leaves the person unprepared and vulnerable to psychic attacks, misinformation and potential traumas.

Life stream: This is the continuous and complete line of every experience and embodiment of the individualism of God which is known as the human Soul. Every human has a Soul, as well as the life giving flame of God in their hearts. There is no power which can strike out that Light of God within. The exacting detail of one's entire life stream: all feelings, thoughts and actions are recorded within the etheric Akashic Records. Every lifestream is reviewed before choosing to re-embody to determine precisely what is needed to further the spiritual development of the Soul in the next embodiment.

Music of the Spheres: Pythagoras, the first Grecian philosopher born between 600 and 590 B.C., is said to have been the only human to actually have heard the music of the spheres in his time on earth. His followers held the belief all that existed also had its special 'voice' in which the praises of their creator were eternally sung and that once mankind had freed themselves from the material illusions of their physical existence based on the senses in favor of the higher realm of the Soul, they would again be able to hear the music of the spheres. The subsequent Greek Mysteries' doctrine included the belief of a profound interconnection between the harmonious musical sound and form which combined to produce an elevated effect upon the listener. In Pythagoras's university at Crotona, this harmonic therapeutic music was written to have cured many physical and spiritual ailments. The music of the spheres was believed to be a healing music, as Archangel Shanuel refers to in the writing titled Transitioning from Earth.

Realms: The realms of existence upon the plane of earth are misunderstood by so much conjecture and psychic discordant information. There is only the realm of life and Light within the heart of every living human on earth. The rest is only mind forms and thoughts which exist only on earth as a result of the composite of mankind's discord and mistaken creation. Once a human being seeks to find the Light within all effects from the discordant realms will no longer be able to touch them in any way. The Angels and cosmic beings of heaven protect the Light in such a way to repel all.

Transition: Death does not exist in the form humanity deems as reality. In truth, there is no death or final passing. The Soul which the Supreme

Being of All Life created lives throughout eternity. The Soul created out of the substance of Light, intelligence and love is the perfect joy of God, Infinite Source. All of creation of the Supreme Being is the joy of love expanding throughout all of the universes of God's creation of all eternal life. Therefore, there is no death or permanent finality to the life God has created: only a transition. Archangel Arazuel is the Being of Light who with infinite love enfolds and carries every Soul during its transition to the heavenly realms where other Beings of Light are present to lovingly assist their acclimation to the higher vibrations of the higher realms where they originally descended from to take on the temporary cloak so to speak of the human form. Archangel Arazuel is the major Being of Light and love who directs the Angelic Host in assisting the transition of every living human upon the planet earth with immense love and unfailing Light to bring them into their true and eternal identity of Light, perfection, love, wisdom and peace. Once the planned earth plane experiences have been accomplished or no longer are feasible the physical plane is left to return to the higher octaves. Transition refers to the complete process of rising above and becoming free once again of the physical plane until the lessons gained in this way are no longer needed and the individual Soul is ready for ascension and permanent residence within the higher octaves of the Ascended Masters, Cosmic Beings and the Angelic Host.

Index

A

Angels 1
aspirations 66

B

Blessing others 11

C

challenges
    God's solution 34
Change
    God's help 59
children
    pregnancy 43
children of the world 41

D

direction and inspiration 67
dreams 44

E

earth 15
energetic system 36
enlightenment 57
expanding love 16

F

feelings 65
finances 39
forgiveness 47

G

God is love 28
God's comforting Light 50
God's grace 30
God's life energy 37, 69
God's Light 17, 58
God's love 4, 24, 31, 48
God's loving direction 3
God's loving will 5
God's perfect love 13, 26
God's presence 32
God's purifying Light 56
God's purifying love 52
God's sources 20
God's wisdom 25, 51, 62
God's wisdom, will and love 60
golden Light of God's wisdom 53

H

healing Light from God 12

About the Author

Being a lifelong learner Stevie Lee Honaker earned a Ph.D. in counseling and career development continuing on to serve in the counseling and career development field within career centers at three large universities and a private college. Now retired from academia, she is devoted to her daily writings which give messages filled with Light, instruction and guidance from the ascended, angelic and beings of Light of the celestial dimensions. These Light beings transmit messages that hold great service and wisdom for assisting mankind. Stevie first began journaling in 1982, when she chose to begin to give her attention to the Lord's Prayer wanting all of its truth and wisdom to fill her heart with complete communion with God. Later she learned she was a claireaudient empath and since then the daily writings from the Angelic Host have expanded to address the problems humanity experience. Everyday another Angel speaks in Stevie's mind the words of love and truth which are meant to uplift and encourage so everyone will have a means of knowing the love of God for all mankind. The Angel's writings offer direct assistance with personal concerns and a way to invite solutions through the Angelic Host into one's daily life. Stevie lives in Colorado; continues to be devoted to the daily writings, has also become a Usui Reiki Master and happily walks her dogs and feeds the many birds that flock to her backyard feeders.